14 DAY EXPRESS PRAYERS FOR EVERYDAY MEN, WOMEN, & TEENS!

Fresh Prayers to Start Your Day — Beginner to Intermediate Version

BY
B5 Publishing, LLC.

I0164420

Allow the potential for growth of your spiritual connection with God in the heavens within 14 days!

Table Of Contents

Introduction

<u>Becoming a Child of God</u>

Becoming a child of God requires giving thanks to our Heavenly Father. You MUST give thanks for the past, present, and the future before you. The past for where you were, the present for how far you've come, and the future for where you're going. Unfortunately, you cannot have your prayers answered without giving thanks to our Father who sacrificed his life on the cross for us. Our Father died for us! He has indeed carried us through to this point in our lives. Even if you feel you haven't had the individual experience of His work through you yet, He's there. Some of us may not see where our Father has carried us, however; through prayer, fasting, meditation, as well as our faith in Christ, you will begin to see through your spiritual eye how far you've come, enlightened by the truth that He is, in fact, there for you. Don't be alarmed when you begin to see things transition right before your eyes. You must believe that the power in prayer our Father has given will begin to manifest—and rather quickly depending on the nature, situation, and position of your calling. Each day before you begin, may each prayer start with "Giving Thanks".

<u>Accepting Christ as Your Lord and Savior</u>

Lord, I give my heart to you. I believe and accept Jesus Christ as my Lord and Savior who sacrificed for my sins and gave His life on the cross for me. Father, speak to my mind, body, soul, and spirit above all things; lead me by the power of the Holy Spirit allowing me the power to experience Your presence and love for all eternity.

<u>Receive Your blessings!</u>

Father, may the expressed prayers within this book allow my relationship with You begin to grow for all eternity. Outstretch Your arm to me, enlarging my knowledge with You ensuring the wisdom and growth of Your Word will give me eternal life. This which will defeat the enemy, prospering me to the Promised Land. As indicated in Hosea 4:6, "My people are destroyed for lack of knowledge: because thou has rejected knowledge, I will also reject thee, that thou shalt be no priest to me: seeing thou hast forgotten the law of thy God, I will also forget thy children. Father, I come not to lack knowledge, as indicated in Hosea 4:6, but to grow in your favor. May these words spoken within your power not have a place in my life as I come to your throne for knowledge, peace, prosperity and purpose" — In Jesus Name.

"Give Thanks"

Heavenly Father, thank You so much for the life You've given for me and my ancestors. Thank You so much for giving the life of Your only begotten Son on the cross as stated in John 3:16. "For God so love the world as to give his only begotten Son, that whosoever believeth in Him shall not perish but may have everlasting life." Father, thank You for the gift of life and purpose given unto me and my ancestors. Thank You for the motivation of others which has allowed me to see through them directly to You. Thank You for making me Your child, delivering me from all evil. Thank you, Father, because of you I am fearfully and wonderfully made. I show appreciation and worship to You for everything You are about to do in my life which will not only change my life for the better but allow me to be a blessing to the lives of many. Thank You, Father, for the gift of discernment and the gift of the Holy Spirit. I worship You. Thank You for strength, favor, purpose, prosperity, resilience, and wisdom. I enter Your gates with praise, worship, boldness, power, and a sound mind in Jesus' mighty name.

<u>Learning "Forgiveness"</u>

Becoming a child of God requires forgiveness. Some of us have sin in our lives which has allowed the enemy, Satan, to secretly judge us for approaching our Father, halting our prayers from being answered. This is a very important part of your daily prayer session in the spiritual realm.

Forgiveness is key. Some of us struggle with forgiveness on behalf of the pain we've endured throughout our lifespan, it's hard! Our Father understands this and has indicated in Romans 12:17-19, "Repay no one evil for evil. Have regard for good things in sight of all men. Beloved, do not avenge yourselves, but rather give place to wrath; for it is written, "Vengeance is mine,

I will repay", says the Lord.

We've all had a hard time forgiving at some point in our lives. I've had a hard time forgiving myself which seemed like the darkest place in my life. After my son was murdered as an innocent bystander to gun violence at the age of nineteen-years-old, I just couldn't pull myself to forgive anyone, not even myself! I couldn't understand why this was happening. He was a freshman in college, funny, beautiful, and strong. He was a hardworking young man who shared partnership in the family business, and just a joy to be around!

So why was this happening to him, to us as family? Our family was there at the scene when it took place, just a few steps from where the shooting transpired. Even his younger siblings ages six, eight, and eleven endured the brutalization of hearing hundreds of gunshots ring off while their brother was in the exact same convenience store buying candy and never came out! It was something out of a horror movie!

All these men, who had nothing to do with our son, my children's brother, suffered through taking the life of my son due to their own negligence, lack of self-control, and most importantly, the lack of our Father Christ Jesus being a part of their lives. Seeing my innocent son slain in the middle of a convenience store floor, lifeless, is unexplainable.

For the men who had no intent

to harm my son, our Father advises us to forgive, and He will repay, right? The dark place almost swallowed me during my time of healing. However, the details of scripture Romans 12:17- 19 in which our Father created for us to follow and abide by, gave me comfort in knowing our Father has created solution beyond anything I could possibly imagine. Our Father, however, didn't allow me go astray. Our Father outstretched his arms and saved me.

And He's ready and willing to save you too.

Please, in the session, take your time. Ask our Father for guidance and strength. He knows our pain. He's ready to forgive us of our debts just as we have to forgive others of their debts, so we can live a life of enjoyment which our Father has promised us. Immediately after giving thanks to our Father, you must ask for the remission (forgiveness) of your sins.

<u>Forgiveness</u>

Heavenly Father I come humbly before Your throne of grace requesting for Your mercy and favor. Father, cover me in the blood of your Son Christ Jesus, forgiving me for all of my sins known and unknown. Father, please forgive me for every negative thought, comment, unholy relationship, negative action, or inappropriate agreement that You have not sanctioned for me.

I ask for forgiveness for entering negative bonds or unholy unions that may have caused You to turn away from me. I stand in agreement on Scripture. 1 John 1:9: that indicates if we confess our sins, You are faithful and just to forgive us of our sins cleansing us from all unrighteousness.

Father, I confess my sins of (Confess your sins! Our Father knows your sins! Don't hold back or hesitate. Be sincere. Our

Father sincerely wants a relationship with you to give you a better life.) Lord, I confess these sins today and accept your forgiveness and cleansing of all unrighteousness. I forgive those who have harmed me in any way just as You have forgiven me. I stand in the gap for my ancestors and plead the blood of Jesus over any sins, known or unknown by them which may have hindered my purpose of your calling through my life in any way as indicated in Jeremiah 32:18, "You show steadfast love to thousands, but you repay the guilt of fathers to their children after them O' great and mighty God whose name is the Lord of the hosts".

I declared that I and my family are redeemed from the hand of Satan by the precious blood of Jesus now and forever as we are forgiven as indicated in Deuteronomy 24:16, "Fathers should not be put to death for their sons, nor shall sons be put to death for their fathers; everyone shall be put to death for his own sin."

Thank you, Lord, for answering my prayers. Thank you for the gift of forgiveness and healing that is now extended to me and my ancestors In Jesus' Mighty Name, Amen

Part 1: Starting Your Spiritual Journey

DAY 1: Allowing God In

After living on edge for most of my life, I decided to allow God in. This wasn't an easy task. No matter how high in life I obtained, I always fell backwards. I always lost in the end. After fighting a battle alone that almost seemed impossible to win, one day I stood up, cried out, and asked for help from God. He was my only source. I was alone in this. Only He could lead me through. After pleading for hours, our Father came to me while sleeping, comforting me. I awoke the next day feeling refreshed, realizing He was there. This is when I begin to "Allow God In."

Meditate On Psalms 24:7, "Lift up your heads, O' ye gates and be ye lift up, ye everlasting doors; and the king of glory shall come in."

Prayer:
Father, I allow you into my life. Sit with me, Father. Fill my spirt with counsel and guidance. Enrich my life and prepare me to be victorious in every situation I face each day. Father, Your Word tells me to call on

You. I call on you, Father; come, enter in!

DAY 2: Approaching the Throne

Allowing God in was most important during my transition to Christ. Standing firm with confidence, not being afraid, I approached His throne. At that time, I was new at getting to know Christ and didn't realize I was approaching His throne spiritually, but I was.

Spiritually, God's throne is a place of power and authority, majesty and honor, perfect justice, sovereignty, holiness, place of praise and purity and eternal life in Heaven. After you allow God in, any time you pray, you are approaching His throne and acknowledging Him.

Meditate on Hebrews 4:16, "Let us therefore come boldly unto the throne of grace that we may obtain mercy and grace in our time of need."

Prayer:
Father, with all Your great mercy, I approach Your throne of grace humbly. I bow to worship You at Your Holy Temple. Surely mercy and goodness should follow me all the days of my life, and I will dwell in the house of the lord forever.

DAY 3: *"Come to Pass"*

Approaching the throne allowed my spiritual eyes to open. My faith grew stronger. I was able to receive discernment (ability to judge well spiritually) through prayer, and my relationship with God grew stronger. The relationship with Christ through prayer request and approaching the throne, created new relationships with family which is where I later found out generational bondages that created curses was definitely the reason behind my rising and falling as indicated In Day 1. Through this knowledge, I was able to defeat the enemy and destroy every curse and generational bondage by regaining control of my work ethics which related to eliminating every form of fear and doubt within me by being confident with who I am, knowing I can accomplish any task before me as long as Christ is with me. Generational bondages in my life have now come to pass.

Meditate on Isaiah 7:7, "Thus, saith the Lord God, it shall not stand, neither shall it come to pass."

Prayer:

I am redeemed from the curse of the law. Father, in Your Name, break all generational curses of witchcraft, perversion, idolatry, confusions, addiction, death, double mindedness, rebellion, pride, fear, and destruction. Father, through your power, I break all spoken curses and negative words over my life, for they shall not come to pass In Jesus' Name.

DAY 4: "Blessings of Favor"

Approaching the throne everyday allowed blessings to begin to flow. One being my family coming together again. I didn't realize spiritual attacks would cause separation, but it did. God is ready to favor you; be ready to receive!

Meditate on Genesis 39:21, "But the Lord was with Joseph, and shewed him mercy, and gave him favor in the sight of the keeper of prison."

Prayer:
Lord, show me your mercy,
releasing your outstretched arm
to me giving me favor and
incredible abundance through
the workings of Your glory.

DAY 5: "Blessings of Favor" (continued)

Meditate On Job 33:26, "He
shall pray unto God, and he will
be favorable unto him. And he
shall see his face with joy for he
will render unto man his
righteousness."

Prayer:
I pray unto the Lord; God grant me favor. Delight me upon my way which may increase all favor submitted to me by you.

DAY 6: Jacob's Prayer Request – "I Will Not Let Go until You Bless Me"

I was strong in my faith. Prayers were being answered. But there was one prayer stubborn enough that it took control of my prayer sessions. I wouldn't stop praying; I just couldn't give up. I would not stop praying until my Father blessed me. It was one day that I finally meditated in my prayer session and listened to God.

The reason behind the blockage? Me. My thoughts, they took over from time to time. I was new at prayer and didn't realize how true it was that God knew my heart. This required more time and diligence so that I could be the person I needed to be in order to receive the prayer request I was asking for. I then began to add to my prayer request advising our Father to renew a right spirit within me, giving me positive thoughts, which I began to see prosper through relationships, my actions as well as my personality.

Meditate on Genesis 32:25-26, "And when he saw that he prevailed not against him, he touched the hollow of his thigh and the hollow of Jacob's thigh was out of joint, as he wrestled with him. And he said, let me go for the day breaketh. And he said, I will not let thee go, except thou bless me."

Bonus Scripture* James 1:17, "Every good gift and every perfect gift is from above, and comes down from the father of lights, with whom there is no variation or shadow of turning."

Prayer:
Lord, you are the Father of lights and the Provider of good gifts. Release the gifts you have assigned upon my spirit into my

life. May today reflect a new start in my life where blessings will be released upon me. In Jesus' Name.

DAY 7: "Finish the Assignment"

To understand the power behind your assignment, you must first approach the throne and advise of the assignment given to you. Don't be afraid or scared if you don't know what your assignment may be. That's what our Father in Heaven is there for; ready and willing to assist. You may approach Him in confidence with a prayer similar to this: "My Father, I thank you for the life that You have given me. I approach Your throne of grace boldly in my time of need. Father, please allow Your Holy Spirit to fill me with my Heavenly purpose here on earth which will make a difference in the lives of many. I live for You, to honor You and walk the path that You have set for me.

Meditate on Nehemiah 2:5, "As

I said to the king, if it pleases the king and if your servant has found favor in your sight, I ask that you send me to Judah, to the city of my father's tomb, that I may rebuild it."

Prayer:
Lord, give me favor like Nehemiah to finish the assignment that You have given me while being protected under the covenant of Your wings. In Jesus' Name.

Part 2: Releasing the Power of

the Father, Son, & the Holy Spirit

DAY 8: "Power of the Enemy"

When your faith become stronger as well as your relationship with Christ, the enemy will try to attack. Don't be alarmed, our Father in Heaven is there and will not allow the enemy to triumph over you. Every time Satan would try to come into my life or family, I would meditate on the Scripture below; even in my prayer sessions which will send the enemy packing faster than he came. Whenever the enemy would try to attack, I would remain confident, standing strong embracing in scripture. Isaiah 4:10 "Fear thou not; for I am with thee: be not dismayed; for I am thy God: I will strengthen thee; yea, I will help thee; yea, I will uphold thee with thy right hand of my righteousness. This scripture allowed comfort in knowing I was not alone and would not be defeated. I would also rest in faith of Christ with scripture Psalm 27:1-3, "The Lord is the light of my salvation; whom shall I fear? The Lord is the strength of my life; of whom shall I be afraid? When the wicked even mine enemies and foes, came upon to eat up my flesh, they stumbled and fell. Though an host should encamp against me, my heart shall not fear: though war should rise against me, in this will confident".

Meditate on Psalms 41:11, "By this I know that thou favourest me, because mine enemy doth not triumph over me."

Prayer:
Because of Your favor, the enemy will not triumph over me. May today be a day of Your protection and glory over me, covering me in Your blood, releasing your power and favor over me unconditionally. In Jesus' Name.

DAY 9: "Looking Forward to the Unseen"

My new business was beginning and with the power of Christ on my side, I had to believe and trust that the family business would prosper and be successful within His timing. Afterall, our Father advises us to look at the bigger picture of where we are today standing in faith trusting His supernatural authority to help us through. I did, and my business picked up in places where I couldn't possibly imagine! We opened a new business building location, we're currently receiving contracts with the government while creating relationships. He has proven his Word is true every time. Remaining faithful even when it doesn't seem as if God is at work in your life will allow our Father to provide blessings within his timing which may not be the time in your life when you are expecting. Rest in knowing our Father is moving at rapid speed to provide you with the blessings you deserve.

Meditate on 2 Corinthians 4:18, "While we look not at the things which are seen but at the things which are not seen are temporal; but the things which are not seen."

Prayer:

Father, may I reap the benefit of the living flow of Your blessings. Surround me, Father, with the supernatural, allowing me to be a giver and receiver of your blessings, removing the burden from giving blessings to others, allowing me as a receiver of blessings to become blessed enough to be a giver as well. In Jesus' name.

DAY 10: "Plans to Follow"

Meditate on Psalms 23, "He restoreth my soul: He leadeth me in the paths of righteousness for his name's sake."

Prayer:
Lord, have mercy on me today, allowing goodness and mercy to follow me all the days of my

life, for You are my Shepherd, and I will not want. I receive the favor of purpose that you have set for me.

DAY 11: "Power of the Tongue"

Each night before I went to bed, I prayed the prayer in which I felt would help me to walk in my purpose. Well, little did I know this prayer would open doors to unimaginable places that would help others walk into their purpose. You see, the power of the tongue is remarkable and can unleash the unthinkable or delay you. Write down your prayers, take your time, and have patience with your tongue; it's your gift to the best place in your life.

Meditate on Psalms 16:11, "Thou wilt shew me the path of life; in thy presence fullness of joy; at thy right hand there are pleasures forevermore."

Prayer:
I will declare to live and not die

and will declare the work of the Lord. Show me the path of life; in Your presence is fullness of joy; at Your right hand are pleasures forevermore.

DAY 12: "Power of Growth through Righteousness"

Continuing my growth through the Christ began to flourish. I looked better, I felt great, my thoughts were outstanding. Even my marriage had begun to flow to another level!

Meditate on Psalms 92:12, "The righteous shall flourish like the palm tree. He shall grow like the cedar of Lebanon."

Prayer:
Father, allow me to flourish just as a beautiful palm tree of fresh Lebanon as your child. Forgive me of my sins, allowing my growth to shine bright where others will see your greatness within me, which will turn them from their wicked ways and allow them to serve you. This

will give man the opportunity to receive your mercy and power as well as greatness, just as I have.

DAY 13: "Blessing of Favor through Redemption"

Meditate on Genesis 39:6, "And he left all that he had in Joseph's hand, and he knew not ought he had save the bread which he did eat. And Joseph was a Godly person and well favored."

Prayer:
Give me favor, Father, in the sight of the world like Joseph. Let me be well favored.

DAY 14: "Favor Unconditionally"

Meditate On Psalms 5:12, "For thou lord wilt bless the righteous with favor wilt thou compass him as with a shield."

Prayer:
Bless me and favor me, Lord.

Surround me with favor like a shield.

Epilogue/Conclusion

Highlights regarding the loss of life of the author and publisher's innocent son slain as an innocent bystander while at work were included to help the reader understand the importance of forgiveness while enduring pain. Accepting Christ as your Lord and Savior, receiving blessings, giving thanks, and requesting forgiveness are all a part of the key factors in obtaining your breakthrough. May each prayer session flow through you in the order submitted within this book to obtain your victory!

Acknowledgments

Inspiration of this prayer book reflects the loss of the author's teenage son who will never marry, have children or get the full experience of the life we all live today as well as the author's sister who, committed suicide within the same year. Having faith in God allowed the author, while receiving God's mercy, be able to stand firm in life again while healing. The author is determined to change lives one step at a time beginning with this prayer book.

<u>Track Your Prayer Request Progress!!!</u>

After every prayer session, monitor your behaviors, thoughts, as well as the people around you. This will help during your alignment (relationship) process with Christ! Write It Down! Use the Day to Day Journal Provided — You can do it!

PART 1 OF YOUR JOURNEY

- ## DAY 1

- DAY 2

- ## DAY 3

• DAY 4

- DAY 5

• DAY 6

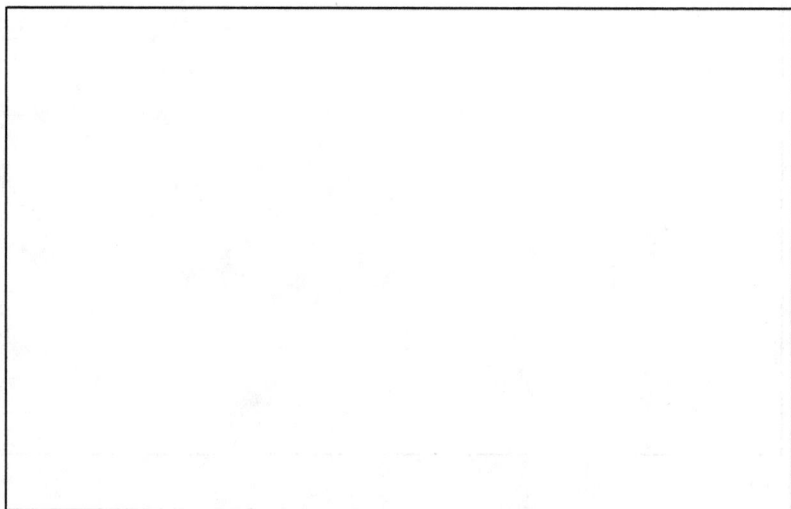

- DAY 7

• DAY 8

• DAY 9

- DAY 10

- ## DAY 11

- DAY 12

- DAY 13

• DAY 14

PART 2 OF YOUR JOURNEY

- DAY 1-2

- DAY 3-4

- DAY 5-6

• DAY 7-8

- DAY 9-10

- DAY 11-12

- DAY 13-14

ADDITIONAL THOUGHTS AND COMMENTS

Tribute

79